The Beak Book

by Robin Page

Beach Lane Books

New York London Toronto Sydney New Delhi

Bird beaks come in many different
colors, shapes, and sizes.
From the time they are born
birds use their beaks—sometimes
called bills—in many unusual
and amazing ways. . . .

This beak is for **straining**.

The duck's soft, flat bill filters seeds, plants, insects, and small animals from the muddy bottom of a pond or river.

ruddy duck

This beak is for sniffing.

The kiwi's nostrils are located at the end of its long beak. This allows it to sniff out earthworms and other underground snacks.

North Island brown kiwi

This beak is for tossing.

The cormorant dives and snags a fish with its hooked beak. Then the bird comes to the surface and flips its prey into its mouth.

double-crested cormorant

This beak is for crushing.

shoebill stork

The shoebill stork's large, heavy beak is perfect for crushing lungfish, catfish, and the occasional lizard or baby crocodile.

This beak is for **cooling.**

keel-billed toucan

The toucan's large beak
radiates heat and cools
the bird on hot days.

This beak is for filtering.

American flamingo

The flamingo turns its beak upside down to filter algae, insects, and shrimp from the water.

This beak is for **snapping.**

roseate spoonbill

As it slashes its spoon-shaped beak back and forth in shallow water, the spoonbill snaps up any prey it touches.

This beak is for stitching.

The mother tailorbird uses her beak to sew a nest for her chicks. She stitches leaves together with spiderweb silk, forming a cozy nest.

common tailorbird

This beak is for **prying**.

red crossbill

The crossbill uses its
unusual beak to pry open
a pinecone and eat the
seeds inside.

This beak is for **stabbing**.

great blue heron

With a quick thrust of its deadly beak, the heron stabs a fish, frog, or other small animal.

This beak is for **ripping.**

The eagle has a powerful hooked beak for ripping its prey into bite-size pieces.

Steller's sea eagle

This beak is for probing.

scarlet ibis

With its slender, curved beak, the ibis probes sandy shorelines and marsh grasses in search of prey.

This beak is for skimming.

Flying just above the surface, the skimmer dips the lower half of its beak into the water to snatch a fish.

black skimmer

This beak is for **plucking**.

South Island takahē

The flightless takahē
(tah-kah-hay) plucks
leaves and grasses with its
short, stout beak.

This beak is for sipping.

The hummingbird hovers
in midair, sipping nectar
with its long, thin beak.

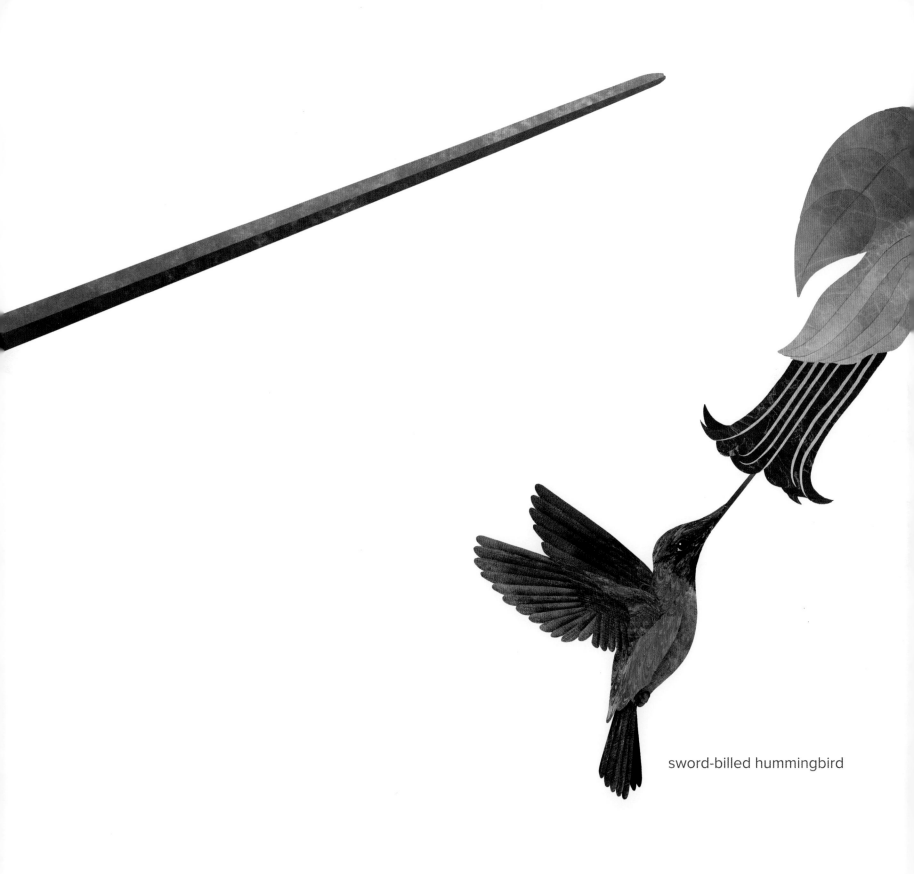

sword-billed hummingbird

This beak is for **climbing**.

hyacinth macaw

The macaw uses its hooked beak to grasp branches as it climbs a tree.

This beak is for **battling.**

Male hornbills use their impressive beaks in mating battles with other males.

oriental pied hornbill

This beak is for **drilling.**

The beak of the woodpecker has a sharp tip that can easily drill into a tree trunk to find the insects hiding beneath the bark.

pileated woodpecker

This beak is for scooping.

Australian pelican

Using the expandable pouch that is part of its beak,
the pelican scoops up a fish.

This beak is for **shredding**.

king vulture

A vulture's hooked beak is the perfect tool for tearing into a dead animal, the bird's favorite food.

This beak is for clutching.

The puffin uses its flexible hinged beak and the sharp spines that line its mouth to clutch several fish at the same time.

Atlantic puffin

This beak is for **tap, tap, tapping...**

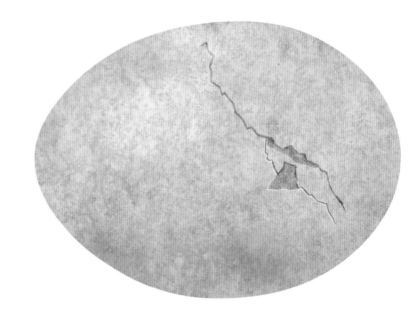

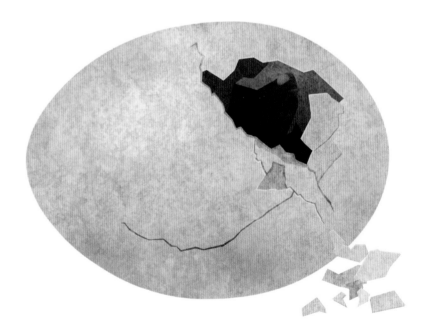

...and **breaking** out of an egg!

Many baby birds use a special egg tooth attached to their beak to break out of their egg. After a while, the egg tooth falls off.

ruddy duckling

Where the birds live and what they eat.

North Island brown kiwi
diet: worms, grubs, insects, berries, seeds, aquatic crustaceans

shoebill stork
diet: fish, amphibians, small reptiles, rodents, other birds

American flamingo
diet: algae, seeds, insects, small aquatic invertebrates

common tailorbird
diet: insects, fruits, berries, seeds

All of the birds are shown at the same relative size, with an adult human for comparison. The yellow areas of the continents show the birds' ranges.*

double-crested cormorant
diet: fish, amphibians, crustaceans, insects

roseate spoonbill
diet: minnows, small crustaceans, insects, plants

ruddy duck
diet: seeds, plants, insects, small aquatic animals

keel-billed toucan
diet: fruits, seeds, insects, eggs, lizards, tree frogs

red crossbill
diet: seeds, berries, insects

*The maps show the typical ranges in which these birds are found.

Steller's sea eagle
diet: fish, birds,
aquatic crustaceans,
carrion

black skimmer
diet: small fish, small
aquatic animals

**sword-billed
hummingbird**
diet: flower nectar,
small spiders,
insects

**oriental pied
hornbill**
diet: fruits, insects,
small birds, reptiles,
amphibians, fish

Australian pelican
diet: fish, crustaceans,
insects, birds

**Atlantic
puffin**
diet: small fish,
small aquatic
animals

great blue heron
diet: small aquatic
animals, small mammals,
birds, insects

South Island takahē
diet: grasses, shoots, insects

pileated woodpecker
diet: insects, fruits, nuts,
berries

scarlet ibis
diet: insects, small
aquatic animals

hyacinth macaw
diet: fruits, nuts, seeds

king vulture
diet: carrion, injured
animals, lizards

Bibliography and Further Reading

allaboutbirds.org

animaldiversity.org

Attenborough, David. *The Life of Birds*. Princeton, NJ: Princeton University Press, 1998.

Ballinger, Emily. *Bird Beaks*. Washington, DC: National Geographic Society, 2004.

Bozzo, Linda. *Amazing Beaks*. New York: Rosen Publishing Group, 2008.

Sen, Moen. *All About Beaks*. New Delhi: Energy and Resources Institute, 2011.

Zommer, Yuval. *The Big Book of Birds*. New York: Thames & Hudson, 2019.

BEACH LANE BOOKS

An imprint of Simon & Schuster Children's Publishing Division
1230 Avenue of the Americas, New York, New York 10020

BEACH LANE BOOKS is a trademark of Simon & Schuster, Inc.
For information about special discounts for bulk purchases, please contact Simon & Schuster Special Sales at
1-866-506-1949 or business@simonandschuster.com.

The Simon & Schuster Speakers Bureau can bring authors to your live event. For more information or to book an event, contact the Simon & Schuster Speakers Bureau at 1-866-248-3049 or visit our website at www.simonspeakers.com.

Book design by Robin Page • Art direction by Irene Metaxatos

The text for this book was set in Arno Pro and Proxima Nova.
The illustrations for this book were rendered in Adobe Photoshop.

Manufactured in China
0422 SCP

2   4   6   8   10   9   7   5   3
CIP data for this book is available from the Library of Congress.
ISBN 978-1-5344-6041-6
ISBN 978-1-5344-6042-3 (eBook)

For Mom—Love, Robin